Xenophobe's®
guide to the
AUSTRIANS

Louis James

D1488026

Xenophobe's Guides

Published by Xenophobe's® Guides
London SW9 7QH

Telephone: +44 (0)20 7733 8585
E-mail: info@xenophobes.com
Web site: www.xenophobes.com

First printed 1994
New editions 2000, 2010
Reprinted/updated: 1997, 1998, 2000, 2002,
2004, 2007, 2010, 2011, 2012, 2013

Editor – Catriona Tulloch Scott
Series Editor – Anne Tauté

Cover designer – Jim Wire & Vicki Towers
Printer – Polestar Wheatons, Devon

Xenophobe's® is a Registered Trademark.

Cover: Austrian cakes by courtesy of
Gloriette Patisserie (Knightsbridge) Ltd.,
London.

ePub ISBN: 9781908120069
Mobi ISBN: 9781908120076
Print ISBN: 9781906042219

Contents

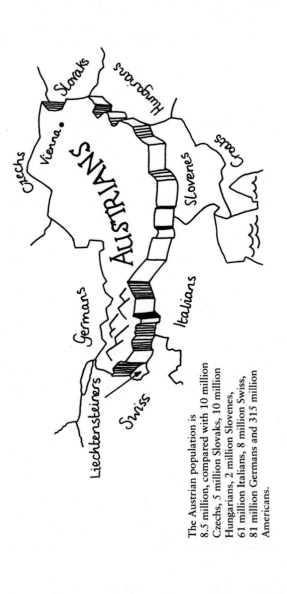

The Austrian population is 8.5 million, compared with 10 million Czechs, 5 million Slovaks, 10 million Hungarians, 2 million Slovenes, 61 million Italians, 8 million Swiss, 81 million Germans and 315 million Americans.

Nationalism & Identity

Forewarned

A great deal of ink has been spilt in Austria agonizing about Austrian identity. Does it actually exist? Should it exist? Is it expanding or diminishing? Is it drawn from the past only, or will it emerge in the future? Hypochondriacs worry about their ailments; Austrians worry about their identity.

> **Hypochondriacs worry about their ailments; Austrians worry about their identity.**

Austrian identity is suspended somewhere between imperial history and parochial loyalties. 'In other countries,' writes an English historian, 'dynasties are episodes in the history of the people; in the Habsburg Empire, peoples are a complication in the history of the dynasty.' The Republic of Austria only came into being in 1918 after the individual nations of the Habsburgs' Austro-Hungarian Empire became independent; as Clemenceau rather brusquely put it: '*L'Autriche, c'est ce qui reste*', i.e. 'Austria consists of what was left over.'

How their neighbours see them

A German historian once remarked a trifle ungraciously that Bavarians were the missing link between Austrians and human beings. He obviously forgot that the ancient Austrians actually came from Bavaria, give

1

or take a few Alemanni.

The German view of Austrians has not mellowed with the passing of time. Hordes of Germans certainly come to beautiful Austria for skiing, hiking and sex; even the large former German Chancellor, Helmut Kohl, used to spend his summer vacation at the Austrian lakes, trying unsuccessfully to lose weight. Unfortunately, this tended to reinforce the image of Austria as a place where you go when you are not being entirely serious, and of the Austrians as a not entirely serious people.

> **66 The Germans feel the Austrians have a tendency to *Schlamperei* (sloppiness or muddle). 99**

The Germans feel that the Austrians have a tendency to *Schlamperei* (sloppiness or muddle), which the locals do not seem to view as a failing. (This characteristic was described by a more tolerant Englishman as 'a sort of laziness, an easy-going spirit which quickly degenerates into slackness. It is shared by the highest and the lowest, causing the former to lose battles, the latter to forget errands.')

The German view of Austrian incompetence is no doubt rooted in history, for the Habsburg armies lost battles to the Prussians with monotonous regularity. The greatest catastrophe was Königgrätz (Sadowa, 1866), when Austrian soldiers rendered every possible assistance to the opposition's artillery by sporting decorative white uniforms, and the Austrian generals could not comprehend why the enemy consistently refused to adhere to the battle plan which they had patiently worked out in elegant manœuvres at home. As one commander plaintively remarked after the defeat: 'It always worked so well on the *Schmelz* (then the military parade and exercise ground in Vienna).' Germans are mystified by the Austrians' delight in telling this story against themselves. To a Prussian, self-irony about military defeats is a self-indulgence only too likely to lead to more of them.

Another German observation concerns the legendary (and largely mythical) Austrian meanness, the implication being that at least one nation is even more careful with money than are the Germans

> **66 The Austrian generals could not comprehend why the enemy consistently refused to adhere to the battle plan which they had patiently worked out. 99**

themselves. A man from München gives a lift home to a Viennese. The Viennese does not offer to pay for petrol; what is more, he demands that they make an enormous detour to include the suburb of a town where he claims to have business. When they get there, it turns out he has 12 returnable bottles in the boot of the car. An advertisement in a Viennese paper had alerted him to the fact that a shop in this suburb pays 5 cents more for empties than anywhere else in Vienna. Seeing the look on the face of his German friend, he hastily offers to pay for the extra petrol. In the end he pays the equivalent of 36 Euros to save 60 cents.

The Hungarians have learnt to regard their neighbours with some affection, particularly the proprietors of cut-price computer shops and used car lots. Budapestians live in daily expectation, or at least hope, of a wall of money from Austrian investors. Border villagers put up signs, with inscriptions in German, advertising hairdressers, dentists and arcane wares.

> **❝ An Austrian marrying into the controlled hysteria of a Hungarian family finds it is just like being at home, only more so. ❞**

Whatever the economic situation, Austro-Hungarian liaisons still occur. The substantial areas of common ground between the two usually ensure that they function well. An Austrian marrying into the controlled hysteria of a Hungarian family finds it is just like being at home, only more so, and a Hungarian finds that his Austrian in-laws cook mountains of heavy, calorie-rich food and force him to eat every scrap of it, just like his mother.

Austrians and Hungarians are not divided by a common language, as are Austrians and Germans, or English and Americans. The Hungarian therefore learns German, which for him is the language of money and career advancement, and charms everybody with his picturesque vowels and quaint Magyar idioms. None of his Austrian in-laws is so foolish as to attempt Hungarian which everyone knows is impossible, and he can thus continue to speak uninhibitedly on the family phone to his dodgy business friends in Budapest.

How they see others

Austrians are deeply ambivalent about the Germans, undecided as to whether they should be portrayed as potential saviours or potential conquerors. It is impossible to ignore entirely the creeping Germanisation of the economy. (Large swathes of the national press and private TV channels are German owned and almost

> **One part of the Austrian psyche is ready to assume that a German scholar carries more weight than an Austrian.**

any Austrian author who wants to make it into 'the big time' hastens to find a German publisher.) Sometimes the Germans have to be humoured and honoured because they offer a solution to a problem. For example, university professorships are frequently offered to German scholars, because internal politicking may have blocked all the viable local candidates. Austrian frustration is compounded by the fact that one part of the Austrian psyche is ready to assume that a German scholar carries more weight than an Austrian, while another part of it thinks of the Germans as *Piefkes* (an abusive term which implies the humourless arrogance of the militaristic Prussian).

The Austrians' other neighbours are the Italians, Slavs, Hungarians and Swiss. With the Italians they would have been able to get along all right had the former not stolen South Tyrol in a shabby deal made with the allies during the First World War. This can be overlooked, however, in view of the fact that Italians have traditionally supplied Austria with composers, architects, divas and ice-cream, all of which are popular. They also supply busloads of tourists. The Viennese shop assistants (who learn useful languages) are past masters at gently assisting linguistically challenged Italian ladies to choose the most expensive items on offer.

> 66 Italians have supplied Austria with composers, architects, divas and ice-cream, all of which are popular. 99

Conversely, ailing North and East Tyroleans were quick to commute across the Italian border when it emerged that some medicines could be up to 40% cheaper in South Tyrol. However, to get medical treatment itself, or have your teeth fixed, the smart solution is to pop over the Hungarian border where white-coated gentlemen and ladies with a felicitous bedside manner are ready and willing to practise their language and other skills on the cost-conscious Austrians.

The situation with the Slavs is more complicated. The Czechs were justifiably annoyed when Emperor

Franz Joseph made a deal with the Hungarians in 1867, creating the Austro-Hungarian Empire. They failed to see why they did not qualify for the same treatment. (Answer: once you start on the Slavs, who knows where it will end?)

Their other Slav neighbours are the Slovenes and the Slovaks. The Slovaks (still sometimes confused with 'Czechs' by people who haven't been paying attention) certainly deserve a mention, which is all they usually get.

> 66 The affinity, or lack of it, that exists between the Austrians and the Swiss is a compound of admiration, envy and contempt. 99

The affinity, or lack of it, that exists between the Austrians and the Swiss is a compound of admiration, envy and contempt. Of course, a lot of people feel that way about the Swiss, but the Austrians have a particular difficulty in concealing their irritation with their neighbours for avoiding conflict and getting insufferably rich – even richer than the Austrians.

The Swiss are not unaware of latent Austrian animosity towards them and try to behave as tactfully as possible. While they cannot actually reduce the number of snow-capped mountains on their territory which compete with Austrian ski resorts, they can at least offer a little discreet banking for what are known picturesquely as *Steuerflüchtlinge* (literally: 'tax fugitives'). When Swiss businesses swallow up Austrian enterprises, as they do from time to time, they adopt an avuncular manner, stressing their alertness to local sensibilities and portraying themselves as responsible partners generously pooling their expertise with Austrian colleagues.

Yet rancorous attitudes persist. In a weekend thin for news, the story was splashed over the Austrian popular press that the roof of the Zürich public baths had fallen in, unfortunately with some loss of life. An elegant lady in a Viennese café reading about the tragedy was heard to murmur, 'At last something has happened to the Swiss.'

How they see themselves

Austria is divided into nine *Länder* (Federal Provinces) which all see themselves as 'Austrian', especially when claiming their share of the Federal Budget.

66 '**Austria', wrote an anonymous pamphleteer in 1841, is a purely imaginary name'. **99**

On the other hand they are defiantly Carinthian, Styrian or Burgenlandian (for example, when asked to help out with the nationwide distribution of asylum seekers or refugees). True, the inhabitants of Salzburg once expressed an overwhelming desire to become part of Germany, and Vorarlberg attempted to slide off into Switzerland; but now everyone has decided to settle down and be Austrian. Or at any rate not something else.

'Austria', wrote an anonymous pamphleteer in 1841, 'is a purely imaginary name'. Moreover, says historian Roman Sandgruber, the word is a philological ragbag since the German root *austr* means 'East', while the Latin *auster* can only mean 'South'. In fact, Austria does not want to be considered an eastern territory (it is bad enough that the Czechs have sneakily located Prague west of Vienna); still less does it wish to be regarded as part of Southern or South-Eastern Europe (it is close enough to the dreaded 'Balkans' already, thank you).

> 66 Any Austrian worth his salt will tell you he is part of Central Europe. Unfortunately no-one knows where 'Central Europe' actually is. 99

Any Austrian worth his salt will tell you he is part of Central Europe; indeed he sees himself as an inhabitant of what was formerly the spiritual and political heart of Central Europe. Unfortunately no-one knows where 'Central Europe' actually was, or is.

The posited location is something of an obsession with Austrians because, as Sandgruber explains, 'Austria draws a good deal of its strength from this idea of the middle, of the centre, of the compromise, exhibiting an almost narcissistic love of the middle way and a levelling of extremes.'

Mere geographical complexities, however, are as nothing compared to the psychological complexities of Austrians as individuals. A Protestant from Tyrol may well exist in a parallel historical reality to a deeply Catholic Lower Austrian, while a second generation Viennese of Slavic origin has nothing in common with Carinthians of German stock who, after nearly a century of disingenuous argufying, are still resisting dual language road signs for villages with mixed ethnicity.

When the celebrated Stone Age man (nicknamed Ötzi) popped out of a glacier in Tyrol in 1991, he was claimed by the Italians as one of them. A learned commission established that maybe he was lying just over the Austrian border by a metre or two, and a television reporter inquired sarcastically why they didn't 'just look at his passport'. The moral of this is: even the ice-man after all those years in cold storage is still as confused about his identity as all other Austrians.

> **66 Collective analysis is not easily applied to the Austrians. 99**

Character

Collective analysis is not easily applied to the Austrians with their mixed Swabian, Bavarian and Slav provenance. As for the Viennese, the complexity of their miscegenation and the resulting contradictions in their character are legendary. Some say they are pleasure-loving, genial and possessed of a 'golden

Viennese heart', while others regard them as devious, morose, time-serving and ill-natured. They can, in fact, be all of these.

The inhabitants of the other provinces seem more homogeneous, exhibiting characteristics determined in part by their situation and/or racial origin. In the Vorarlberger and the Tyrolese, for instance, one can recognise Swiss-type qualities of diligence, thrift, piety and stubbornness. Local patriotism is intensely strong amongst the hot-blooded Carinthians in the south, whose notorious chauvinism is not unconnected with the presence of a sizeable Slovene minority.

> **Austrians continue to live in several diverse traditions and are thus capable of taking up different positions simultaneously.**

As a result of the languages, characteristics and multifarious *Weltanschauungen* (ways of looking at the world) that comprise the collective notion of 'Austrians', they continue to live in several diverse traditions and are thus capable of taking up different positions simultaneously. (It was an Austrian who set up the first Institute for the Study of Conflict and another, Richard Coudenhove-Kalergi, who first articulated the quaint idea of a Pan-European Union achieved by consent, not force.)

Other traits of the Austrian character that overleap provincial borders date back to the Metternich era (1814-1848) when conformity was imposed upon the whole population with an iron fist. Conformance on the one hand and a strategy of 'inner emigration' on the other became the traditional survival techniques adopted by Austrians when faced with *force majeure*.

Inner emigration

Avoiding unpleasantness with the authorities has encouraged the dominance of presentation over substance. By the same token, the Austrians have two existences, one for the bureaucratic files and one for actual use. They have become past masters of parallel realities.

> **In Austria detonating pretension is a national pastime.**

One consequence is that the Austrian character acquires a veneer beneath which frustration and resentment can grow; and here lies the root of the Austrian's ambivalent attitude to power, the mixture of obsequiousness and rancid contempt with which he approaches all who to him appear high and mighty. In Austria detonating pretension is a national pastime, one that can be enjoyed by all for the simple reason that the pretensions are there to be detonated. The playwright Franz Grillparzer who was in many ways the Austrian par excellence, a grumpy genius with a safe job in the state sector, remarked that his fellow-countrymen 'held greatness to be dangerous and fame an empty vanity'.

This opinion seems to have been ingrained in Austrians even before the collapse of their great empire. It has to do with attitudes to power that date back to an absolutist form of government and with the self-irony developed by people who were (or thought they were) more talented than the authority to which they had to defer. It has made the Austrians a fascinating mixture of the predictable and unpredictable, by turns kindly and malicious, steadfast and devious, over-confident and under-confident. It has made Austria a place where saloon-bar arrogance suddenly evaporates into spiritual humility and an over-developed sense of the ridiculous threatens genuine achievement and charlatanism alike.

> **An over-developed sense of the ridiculous threatens genuine achievement and charlatanism alike.**

It behoves the outsider to tread carefully in this hall of mirrors, where all generalisations are as true as their opposites. Or, as Austrian dramatist and comedian Johann Nestroy characteristically put it, 'I'd like to have a real go at myself once in a while, just to see which is stronger: me or myself.'

Conservatism versus creativity

The paradoxical character of the Austrian mingles profoundly conservative attitudes with a flair for innovation and invention. This creative tension usually takes the form of official obstructionism to good ideas, but sometimes the other way round. For example,

> **" The Austrian needs lots of persuading to have his traditions tampered with in the name of modernisation and efficiency. "**

the population were outraged by Emperor Joseph II's attempt to make them adopt re-usable coffins with flaps on the underside for dropping out the corpses. (He was forced to back down, grumbling as he did so about the people's wasteful attitude.)

Rigid conservatism is blamed for what is gleefully described as the *österreichische Erfinderschicksal* – the supposedly typical Austrian fate of being ignored if you come up with a new invention. The powers-that-be, or their bureaucratic subordinates, are said to ward off unwelcome innovation using one of three possible lines of defence:

'*Das hamma noch nie gemacht*' – 'We've never done that' (and we're not about to start);

'*Das hamma immer schon so gemacht*' – 'We've always done it that way' (and are not about to change); or

'*Da könnt ein jeder kommen*' – 'Then anyone could come along' (and tell us to implement some footling idea like yours).

The Austrian needs lots of persuading to have his traditions tampered with in the name of modernisation and efficiency. He is attached to the religious holidays that bespatter the calendar, highly anachronistic in a world where workers get generous holiday allowances. He is attached also to his sausage, his insipid beer, and the young white wine that tastes so remarkably like iron filings. He prefers the familiar, tried and tested to novelty, the latter almost certainly being an attempt by persons unknown to make money at his expense.

Then again, he can equally well be open to new ideas and correspondingly impatient with the cant pumped out on behalf of vested interests and indolent reaction.

Janus-headed, the nation often seems to be looking backward even as it moves forward, and vice versa. Its hallmark is maintaining a certain ironic distance from the dead hand of the past

> **He is attached to his sausage, his insipid beer, and the young white wine that tastes so remarkably like iron filings.**

and the claims of the future, such scepticism being appropriate to the inquiring Austrian mind. Thus one half is work mad, and the other half is all too aware of the vanity of human endeavour.

'Why are all these people running like hell?' goes a local joke. 'They're competing in a marathon,' comes the answer. 'But why are they competing?' 'Because the one who comes first gets a big prize.' 'OK. But why are all the others competing?'

Attitudes & Values

Status

The Austrian's quest for stability takes the form of a nostalgia for hierarchies that once determined man's place from the highest to the lowest rung on the social ladder. Until the removal of the Habsburg dynasty in 1918, the court remained the fount of all patronage. To get on in life you needed *Protektion*, i.e. a person who would recommend you for advancement. This is the origin of the Austrian obsession with titles and forms of address, which perform the twin functions of boosting your status in the eyes of those around you and of flattering the person who (you hope) will advance your interests.

> **66 Although all noble titles have long been banned by law, there is a seemingly unending list of professional titles to choose from. 99**

Although all noble titles have long been banned by law, there is a seemingly unending list of professional titles to choose from. The most engagingly baroque handles were to be found in the Civil Service with titles like *Hofrat* (Aulic Councillor – the Aulic Council was founded in 1498). Several of 19 such titles listed in the Civil Service Directory of 1910 are still in use today. Though the outsourcing of state activities to the private sector is gradually eroding these formal rankings, the term *Hofrat* is likely to remain part of an Austrian's mental furniture for generations.

Formal address, by title rather than by name, stretches downwards as well as upwards in Austria. It is claimed that government chauffeurs can attain the dizzy rank of *Fahrmeister* ('driving master'), provided they survive a few years in the job without any spectacular crashes.

As with bureaucrats, so with academics, whose various grades of achievement have been punctiliously observed over the years: time was when, as the Rector of a *Hochschule* (any institute of higher learning), you would have been

> **" Grades of achievement are punctiliously observed: time was when, as the Rector of a *Hochschule*, you would have been addressed as Your Magnificence. "**

addressed as *Eure Magnifizenz* – Your Magnificence. Should you reach the status of *Dozent* (university lecturer), you could then aspire to a Professorship, but this will only be 'Extraordinarius' (Associate) unless you manage to bag a Chair. The latter position is of such eminence that hall porters (the most acute barometers of social standing in Austria) project waves of sycophancy at your person as you pass, and a faint but detectable halo glimmers above your head when you deign to address the nation from a television studio.

Women professors are a rare species, so do not be fooled by the courtesy title '*Frau Professor*' which is acquired by the wives of professors through a process of social osmosis. The osmosis does not work in the other direction however, for in the male chauvinist world of Austrian academe there is no way the socially crushed husband of a *Frau Professorin* could get away with styling himself *Herr Professor*.

It is possible to bypass the snakes and ladders of professional (and social) advancement by going into business and getting rich. When you have made it, you demonstrate the fact by building a villa in a favoured area for an astronomic sum (this was the undoing of one Vice-Chancellor, whose ostentatious villa provoked the Revenue to inquire into the source of his funds). If the villa is not considered prestigious enough on its own, you can always buy an Honorary Consulship for some obscure African country to go with it. The work is not taxing and the representation looks good on your notepaper.

> **❝An important status symbol is the motor car. Even families with limited means usually buy the most prestigious car they can possibly afford. ❞**

An important status symbol is the motor car – in particular Mercedes, Audis and BMWs. Even families with limited means usually buy the most prestigious car they can possibly afford, while *Gastarbeiter* (foreign guest workers) traditionally invest in the larger Mercedes models, second-hand (sometimes very second-hand), for roaring back and forth between their homelands and Vienna, always with a full complement of family and most of the family assets.

All Austrians are experts on the price of cars. For this reason possession of the appropriate German model is a statement of net worth readily comprehensible to inferior beings such as Lada drivers and pedestrians.

Wealth and success

The attitude of the average Austrian to money and success is at best ambivalent. Envy has something to do with this, but there is also a deep-rooted scepticism (based on what the man on the Vienna tram fancies he knows about the workings of the system). If somebody steps into the limelight, the first question everyone asks is: 'Who is behind him?'

> **If somebody steps into the limelight, the first question everyone asks is: 'Who is behind him?'**

Of course he may have got where he has through talent and energy; on the other hand, as all properly informed persons will hasten to tell you, there are dozens of others equally or better qualified for the job.

There is a great deal of truth in this view. Austria is a small country with a generally highly educated population and it is unlikely that there will ever be enough top jobs to mop up all the able people. 'Who you know' is inevitably just as important as 'what you know'. Thwarted ambition is thus a chronic condition for a substantial and vocal sector of the population.

Relative paucity of opportunity and the continual necessity to guard one's rear have in the past led to a 'winner takes all' tendency in public life which increases the cynicism of ordinary mortals. There is even a phrase for it, *Ämterkumulierung* (job accumulation, a euphemism in most cases for 'salary accumulation'). When political muckraking exposed the National Bank for having doubled as a honey pot for politically correct appointees, it transpired that the Governor received a salary which made that of the Head of the Federal Reserve in New York look like pin-money. More than one director was receiving princely remuneration for no visible contribution to the deliberations of the bank, and those who were asked to clear their desks in the wake of the furore may have had difficulty remembering where their desks actually were.

> **66 Thwarted ambition is a chronic condition for a substantial and vocal sector of the population. 99**

A people who have been on the losing side in two world wars, endured a civil war, hyper-inflation and several spectacular stock-market crashes, all within the last three generations, may be forgiven for exhibiting a certain caution in their modus operandi. This may help to explain why Austrians remain the world's most fanatical savers, accumulating billions in accounts which often pay pitiful rates of interest.

Until European Union rules banned the anonymous nature of *Sparbücher* (savings books), they were the preferred form of saving for the majority of Austrians, despite being an astonishingly bad deal. Although the interest was taxed at source and therefore the gain from the interest undeclared on the tax return tended to be minimal, the *Sparbuch's* anonymity (no name

> **❝ Austrians are the world's most fanatical savers, accumulating billions in accounts which often pay pitiful rates of interest. ❞**

was used, just a password) was a potent symbol of Mr. Average Austrian's pride in his imagined shrewdness – and of the banks' glee in taking advantage of it.

Immigrants

The Austrians' Southern Slav neighbours are encountered mainly in the shape of *Gastarbeiten* (guest workers), who are concentrated in Vienna, where they are employed in the construction and service industries. Nearly 19% of the population of Vienna (where one-fifth of the Austrian population live) are foreigners. The largest number (nearly half) come from the lands of the former Yugoslavia. Rather surprisingly, Germans constitute the next largest group of immigrants (many

Germans study in Austria because of a quota system operated in German universities, especially for the medical schools.) Then come Turks and Poles, with a further large number of people from the former Communist states to the East who are gradually gaining legal access to Austrian jobs since their countries joined the E.U. Many of these incomers have been working and paying taxes in Austria for years and the Employers' Federation is among their stoutest supporters.

66 The black economy is something of which most Austrians tacitly approve, at least if it means getting that window fixed at half the going rate. 99

However suspicion about the actual activity of 'foreigners', whether justified or not, is grist to the mill of extreme right politicians who benefit from scare campaigns about mafias, drug peddling and the black economy. This last, however, is something of which most Austrians tacitly approve, at least if it means getting that window fixed at half the going rate.

Some anti-foreigner feeling can be heard in bars, where there are mutterings about the *Tschuschen* (an insulting term for Balkan peoples) who are a familiar sight at the Südbahnhof (the railway station for the south) with their *Tschuschen-Koffer* (Tschuschen suitcases, i.e. plastic bags). All the same, the Austrians acknowledge that these industrious people do the dirty jobs that they themselves have become too grand to do.

The Czechs supplied most of the brickmakers (known as *Ziegelbehm* or 'Bohemian brickies') in 19th-century Vienna. The natives' view of their habits is reflected in words like *tschechern*, meaning to drink (alcohol, and copiously) and *Tschecherl,* the term for a greasy spoon or sleazy diner. The Czechs have supplied the Austrian cuisine with its best item – dumplings. The entirely inoffensive Emperor Ferdinand, who was sent away to Prague after his enforced abdication, reportedly made one remark that gave the lie to his alleged simple-mindedness, namely, 'I am the Emperor and I shall have dumplings.'

> **"Emperor Ferdinand reportedly made one remark that gave the lie to his alleged simple-mindedness, namely, 'I am the Emperor and I shall have dumplings.'"**

Although there are some problems with schools that are flooded with immigrant children, the age-old Viennese absorption mechanism is at work – for instance, through Austrian education Slav children become bilingual and are then indistinguishable from their counterparts in history who underwent the same process – and whose names fill the Viennese telephone book. (As early as 1787 it was stated that no Viennese family 'could trace its indigenousness further back than three generations'.)

The cabaret artist Hugo Wiener illustrated this assimilation process in a sketch which is set in an office of the Aliens Bureau where two officials are interviewing a Turk for extension of his residence permit. With elaborate pantomime and pidgin German they convey various questions: Is he married? Does he work? Where does he live? It is clear the Turk has difficulty in understanding the frequently misleading pantomime, and the questions with their broken syntax. At length another official arrives, and unaware of what has been going on, asks the Turk the same questions very rapidly in German with a Viennese dialect. To the astonishment of the first two officials the Turk answers equally rapidly and at considerable length in faultless German. 'Gracious!' exclaims one of the officials, 'And there we were trying to make things easy for him by explaining everything in Turkish.'

> **In Austria piety co-exists with wealth in a manner calculated to do minimal injury to the image of either.**

Religion

In Austria, as in other Catholic countries, piety co-exists with wealth in a manner calculated to do minimal injury to the image of either. Citizens are reminded of their obligations to the church by the existence of a church tax. This is levied on the principle that you pay it automatically unless you take the trouble to opt out. Panic broke out in the senior echelons of the church when the Association of Taxpayers began questioning the desirability, and even the ethics, of maintaining such a system. Bishops appeared on television to explain the good work the church does in the field of charitable provision and the preservation of monuments. Their entirely truthful protestations cannot quite conceal the root of the problem – the rising unpopularity of an institution that takes no notice of half a million of the faithful who

66 Citizens are reminded of their obligations to the church by the existence of a church tax. 99

have asked for participation in the appointment of bishops, the ordination of women priests, the abolition of enforced priestly celibacy and a 'positive evaluation' of sexuality on the part of the church.

For centuries the faithful divided their abundant reserves of obedience between church and dynasty. Where their consciences compelled them to reject the official line, they adopted the tactic of inner emigration – and thereby escaped from ideological conflict into 'happiness in a quiet corner' of private life. However a new spirit is abroad in the 'Isle of the Blessed', as Austria was once smugly described. Pope John Paul II's policy of packing the church hierarchy with reactionary bishops dramatically backfired. A scandal concerning no lesser person than the Cardinal

25

Archbishop of Vienna involving boys formerly in his care proved to be the final straw for many liberal Catholics. When the accusers began to multiply alarmingly, the church at first went into denial, following an ancient ecclesiastical principle: '*Was nicht sein darf, nicht sein kann*' ('What may not happen, cannot have happened'), and the gentleman in question was smuggled off to a nunnery in Germany.

The replacement Cardinal Archbishop embarked upon a process of damage limitation, but it's an uphill struggle. 87,000 people left the Catholic Church in Austria in 2010 in the wake of paedophile scandals which is equivalent to the entire population of St. Polten (the capital of Lower Austria). The situation is so bad that the Salzburg diocese even employs a missionary to try and lure people back.

> **Home life for the Austrians is a never-ending quest for *Gemütlichkeit* or cosiness.**

Behaviour

The domestic idyll

Home life for the Austrians is a never-ending quest for *Gemütlichkeit* or cosiness, which is achieved by accumulating objects that run the gamut from the pleasingly aesthetic to the mind-blowingly kitsch. The clutter is often sunk in a Stygian gloom, considered soothing and dignified by the proprietors, but which may make it difficult for a guest to locate his host, or even to see what he is eating. While this is typical of old-style, middle-class living, modern apartments tend to veer towards the other extreme, exuding a brittle cheerfulness enhanced by pastel colours and pine furniture from IKEA.

The average Austrian housewife is house-proud to the point of obsession. Slippers are provided for visitors so that they do not dirty the carpets which have been hoovered into a state of abject submission. Dust is conspicuous by its absence and lavatories and baths gleam smugly as in advertisements for household cleansers. Children are permitted a certain amount of disorder in their rooms, but otherwise tidiness rules: pots, pans, glasses, tools, books, etc., have a primary function, that of being in their right place, which often seems to overwhelm their secondary function, that of being taken down and used.

> **Slippers are provided so that visitors do not dirty the carpets which have been hoovered into a state of abject submission.**

Ideally, perfect harmony is achieved between *Ordnung* (order) and *Gemütlichkeit*: in such a world no-one drops ash on the carpet and the lavatory paper never runs out. Mr. and Mrs. Austria perch happily in this never-to-be-fouled nest, making love and rearing their chicks in the time left over from cleaning and polishing.

Children

Austrian attitudes to children, as to so much else, appear to be contradictory. If the Austrian psychiatrist Erwin Ringel were to be believed, many children are permanently damaged by authoritarian attitudes, prudery about sexual matters and other parent-inspired ills. But anyone with first-hand experience of an Austrian family and its demanding offspring will have difficulty believing this, for authoritarianism has largely given way to liberalism.

> **66** Austrian senior citizens are capable of subjecting babies to admiration of the sort that would look excessive coming from the Madonna. **99**

In fact, Austrian parents spend more money per capita per child per annum on toys than parents in any other European nation. As no-one has yet suggested that most of these toys are really for parental consumption, one must assume that children are the beneficiaries.

The elderly

Austrian senior citizens may glare at rowdy children on trams and buses, but they are also capable of subjecting babies to uncritical admiration of the sort that would sound excessive coming from the Madonna. (However, this could be said merely to demonstrate the older generation's preference for the *unmündig*

28

over the *mündig*, i.e. for those who can't answer back over those who can.) Whether it is the final pay-off for the toy glut, or because of deeply ingrained social codes, Austrians tend to look after the aged and are somewhat less inclined to shove them into homes as happens elsewhere.

But having a resident *Besserwisser* (know-all) discoursing easily and well on the right and the wrong way to bring up chil-

> **66 If you don't keep a grandmother in Austria, you may well keep a dog or a cat. 99**

dren inevitably leads to a certain amount of friction in the home. Since Austrian men dare not oppose their mothers openly, their wives are usually left to face this battle of wills alone. Social taboos will usually ensure suppression of rage in the domestic sphere, but persons in public life who have outstayed their welcome enjoy no such immunity: terms of abuse include *alter Trottel* (elderly moron), and the picturesque *Grufti* (one who has escaped from the tomb).

Animals

If you don't keep a grandmother in Austria, you may well keep a dog or a cat. Canine pets have reached such numbers in Vienna that up to 10 tons of fæcal matter are deposited daily on the city streets.

To get to grips with the problem, a Parisian firm was once summoned to Vienna to demonstrate its hit squad of orange-suited, motorised shit collectors going about their business. The mayor himself accompanied them as they flashed round the town vacuuming dog messes. However, it was quickly sensed that Viennese burghers would not take kindly to being terrorised on the pavements by whirlwind Dirty Fido operatives. A truly democratic solution to dog shit has yet to be found but the patriotic Viennese do assiduously collect their dogs' leavings in dinky little plastic or paper cornets.

> **A special place in Austrian affections is reserved for the horse.**

A special place in Austrian affections is reserved for the horse; not that many people can afford to keep one, but horses have traditionally been seen to lend extra dignity to humans, especially emperors and generals. The most famous Austrian horses are, of course, the Lipizzaners, who perform a ballet-like dressage in the Spanish Riding School of Vienna's Hofburg. These beautiful white beasts enjoy all the cosseting befitting an Austrian state employee, i.e. generous holidays and an Indian summer of handsomely pensioned tranquillity.

As one of the country's biggest foreign currency earners their cachet is rivalled only by that of the Vienna Philharmonic and the Vienna Boys' Choir. Lipizzaners would seem to have realised every man's dream of achieving social prestige combined with job security. No wonder it was the boast of one Mayor of Vienna, that many little Austrians 'want to be members of the Vienna Boys' Choir in their youth and Lipizzaner stallions when they grow up'.

Queuing

The ability or inability to queue marks the difference between the 'European' and the 'Balkan' mentality. That the Balkans lie on the doorstep may be deduced from the Austrians' way of queuing, the art of which they have nearly mastered, but not quite.

The average Austrian does stand in line, demonstrating his European side, but his preference is to edge forward until he is level-pegging with the person in front. He always seems to be on the point of barging the queue, but never actually does. Apart from inducing a state of nervous agitation in the person ahead of him, this is a relatively harmless manoeuvre, except in banks. Here the cashiers have felt obliged to paint two yellow footprints a couple of metres short of the teller's window and to display a notice which states that, in the interests of client confidentiality, no-one should overstep the footprints until it is their turn to be called. Since all Austrians like to guard their privacy with a zeal

66 The average Austrian always seems to be on the point of barging the queue, but never actually does. 99

bordering on an obsession, this is a message even compulsive queue-edgers are prepared to respect.

Driving

The unbridled aggression of the average Austrian driver may partly be due to the frustrating road conditions in his small country, but it also seems to be a character trait. If you obey the speed limit, you will soon have a purple-faced Opel ogre on your back bumper, flashing his lights. If you signal to filter across the lines on a ring road, as likely as not a Mercedes mugger will accelerate from behind to block your passage.

> **The unruffled businessman, the mild and courteous burgher, even the fawning waiter is suddenly a caveman on wheels.**

The principal tactics of the nation's road-hogs are cutting in while pretending that his victim is the one failing to observe lane discipline, horn-blowing as soon as the lights turn to green, and light-flashing at all and sundry.

As soon as he gets behind the steering wheel, the Austrian male is transformed from mouse to monster. The unruffled businessman, the mild and courteous burgher, even the fawning waiter is suddenly a caveman on wheels. The highway is where the Austrian feels he has a licence to blow off steam and show the world that, however much he may be humiliated and pushed about at the workplace or hen-pecked at home, there is still a little corner of his soul that is for ever Arnold Schwarzenegger.

Manners

Greetings and forms of address

Austrians are sticklers for formal manners. Hand-shaking is a national pastime and latecomers to committee meetings hold up proceedings until all available flesh has been pressed; and woe betide anyone who fails to greet, whether entering a shop or buying a postage stamp.

The usual Austrian greeting is the South German '*Grüss Gott*', but the socialist-inclined, who are careful to leave God out of the matter, greet with '*Guten Tag*'. There

> **66 An ascending scale of deferential verbal approaches ranges from 'My deep respect', through 'My reverence' to 'My devotion'. 99**

are flattering forms of address which can be employed either ironically, or as a perfectly genuine display of courtesy. An ascending scale of deferential verbal approaches ranges from 'My deep respect', through 'My reverence' to 'My devotion'. From time to time one receives letters that close with an expression of regard to one's 'revered wife' and sign off with a flourish such as 'Your devoted...' These formulas have their origin in the etiquette books of the early 19th century and in the nuances of the social pecking order under the Austro-Hungarian Empire.

> ❝ A sideways motion of the bowed head a few centimetres above the hand in question is considered more than adequate. ❞

Increasingly archaic, though occasionally still witnessed, is the chivalrous approach to women with the words '*Küss die Hand*' (I kiss your hand), but it is not always well received if you actually proceed to do so. A sideways motion of the bowed head a few centimetres above the hand in question is considered more than adequate and avoids the humiliation of having it abruptly withdrawn just before labial impact.

Other somewhat outmoded forms of address have also entered the province of irony, largely due to their merciless exploitation by cabaret artists and the tidal waves of feigned deference emanating from Viennese waiters, such as '*Gnädiger Herr*' – Your Lordship, '*Habedieehre*' – May I have the honour, and '*Gschamsterdiener*' – Your most obedient servant. '*Gnädige Frau*' – Gracious Lady or Madam, can be either ironic or sincere according to context.

Young people and intimates dispense with formal greetings and leave-takings, contenting themselves with '*Servus*', '*Grüss Dich*' and (in Vienna) '*Papa*'.

This informality should not lead one to suppose that the act of greeting has become any the less important. Not to greet is regarded as a personal affront and there are few greater solecisms that an Austrian can commit. In a hostile obituary of the Archduke Franz-Ferdinand after the latter's assassination in 1914, the most damning indictment of the man who indirectly caused the First World War was the accusation: '*Er war kein Grüsser...*' ('He didn't greet ...').

Etiquette

The prelude to an Austrian dinner is often a glass of fruit *Schnaps*, which should be tipped down the throat in a single motion. As this is drunk on an empty stomach, it has an effect roughly equivalent to throwing paraffin on the living-room fire and is considered a satisfactory method of kick-starting the evening's entertainment. Austrians are used to these preliminaries and show no reaction beyond a slightly enhanced glitter of the eyeballs.

> **Not to greet is regarded as a personal affront and there are few greater solecisms that an Austrian can commit.**

Another important point of drinking etiquette arises once you are seated at the table. Nobody is allowed to drink until the host has raised his glass and toasted the company '*Prost, zum Wohl*'. Lashing into the wine without waiting for this ritual will attract incredulous looks, even if, as sometimes happens, the host is so busy holding forth that he has forgotten to fire the starting-gun. An absent-minded sip may attract the softly spoken comment: 'Are we drinking English-style tonight?' which at least reminds the host of his duties, but does nothing for the *amour-propre* of the guilty party.

> **66 Austrians are used to heavy food and can despatch astonishing quantities of it very rapidly and in a manner that may be said to display grace under pressure. 99**

The green light for eating usually takes the form of a similar verbal ritual – '*Guten Appetit*' or '*Mahlzeit*' (enjoy your meal) – but after that you're on your own, literally so in the case of many foreigners, for Austrians are used to heavy food and can despatch astonishing quantities of it very rapidly and in a manner that may be said to display grace under pressure.

Even outside the realm of social eating and drinking Austrian manners remain disciplined and orderly. Formality is still cultivated among the older genera-tion, and admission into a relationship of intimacy, i.e. the switch from *Sie*, the formal 'you', to *du*, the informal one, can only be initiated by the elder of the people concerned. (When the magic moment comes, he may raise his glass to you and pronounce his Christian name; you respond in kind and thereafter need have no further worry about revealing your tax evasion scheme in his presence.)

A woman is more likely to announce: 'We are now on *du* terms', while the younger generation have mostly shortened the incubation period for the birth of a *du* relationship to a few meetings, or even a few hours. Youth culture has introduced the commercial use of the *du* form, so that your internet server, or indeed anyone trying to sell you some trendy product like an iPod, will also use *du*. In environments that constitute a sort of *de facto* freemasonry, such as the students' canteen in the university, there is a tendency to dispense with *Sie* altogether. On the other hand, colleagues who have spent a lifetime working at neighbouring desks may adhere ostentatiously to the *Sie* form, especially if they dislike each other.

> 66 The keynote of Austrian humour is retrospective pessimism, a conviction that things turn out badly, even when they turn out well. 99

Sense of Humour

The keynote of Austrian humour is retrospective pessimism, a dearly clung-to conviction that things turn out badly, even when they turn out well; this is the refined Austrian version of the famous Italian insight: 'We were better off when we were worse off.'

Austria's history is the soil that nurtured a humour of damage limitation or graceful resignation, one that pours the balm of self-mockery on the wounds of small and great defeats. The attitude was admirably summed up by an Austrian general, who reacted to the approach of yet another military catastrophe with the airy observation: 'The situation is hopeless, but not serious.'

> **66 Austria's history is the soil that nurtured a humour of damage limitation or graceful resignation. 99**

The Austrian favours wit and irony, rather than the pun. Wit is employed to invent wonderfully vivid names, a skill developed to the highest degree by the comedian and playwright Nestroy, whose works are littered with creations such as *Lumpazivagabundus*, a word concocted from *Lump* (meaning a scoundrel) and vagabond.

Viennese dialect is particularly rich in vividly descriptive coinages such as *Grabennymphen* (Graben nymphs), a term for prostitutes dating from the time they thronged the Graben which is now the most fashionable street in Vienna. (It is said that Count Taaffe, when he was Prime Minister, on taking a post-prandial stroll there, noted with surprise the absence of the *Nymphen*. His companion, a municipal official, explained that they had been cleared into the back streets because their very great number made it 'no longer possible to distinguish honest women from the tarts'. 'Maybe you and the police can't,' observed Taaffe drily, 'but the rest of us manage it perfectly well.')

Viennese humour is variously distilled from the sly surrealism of the Czechs, the gallows wit and professional pessimism of the Hungarians, and the Italian tradition of clowning and mimicry. Jewish writers and cabaret artists have also contributed their own brand of acerbic observation, the threatened underdog's traditional tactic for deflecting aggression.

Defensive wit is an enduring element in the Austrian's rueful view of the world and his own diminished place in it. Irony puts the great in their place, but also permeates the average Austrian's view of himself, which is much the same thing as his *Weltanschauung*. 'The Austrian tends to navel-gazing,' remarks a contemporary politician, 'by which I mean he sees in himself the whole world.'

The Austrian's depiction of himself as a self-absorbed bit-player on the great stage of life constitutes a leitmotif of the nation's humorous self-perception. It is seen as much in Nestroy's famous claim: 'Success decides nothing', as it is in a contemporary graffito scrawled on the interior of a Viennese tram: 'Knowledge pursues me but I am faster!'

> **“ Defensive wit is an enduring element in the Austrian's rueful view of the world and his own diminished place in it. ”**

Yet the Austrian capacity for self-denigration has a

harsh and bitter side, and even as the outsider begins to explore the possibility that all this persiflage conceals a darker truth, he finds the Austrian has got there first. 'I expect the worst from everybody, including myself,' said Nestroy, 'and I am seldom disappointed.'

Obsessions

Apart from their relatively modern obsession with motor cars (one should not forget that Ferdinand Porsche and Niki Lauda are among Austria's most illustrious sons), Austrians have two enduring obsessions: collecting and death.

Collecting

Collecting may be traced back to the Habsburgs who accumulated new territories, titles and treasures as lesser men collect stamps. Few Austrians can afford to collect as they did, but one contemporary collector, the ophthalmologist Rudolf Leopold, accumulated such a store of priceless Klimts, Schieles and other works by major Austrian painters that an entire building was reserved for it in a new museum complex, and Leopold himself was appointed director for life. (The story goes that his family once begged him to take a picture to Sotheby's in London in order to raise much-needed cash. Eventually he was persuaded, went to London and sold the picture. Then, with the proceeds, he bought another.)

Happily for the ordinary Austrian there are lots of more affordable substitutes to collect. Kitchen walls are plastered with folk pottery from surrounding countries and living rooms are filled with assiduously collected souvenirs from holidays abroad – a gondolier on a glass boat, three different sizes of cow-bell, and a donkey with a nodding head. Sometimes entire rooms are turned into display units, like the man who had over 500 coffee pots lining the walls of his living room from floor to ceiling, and who went each Saturday to the fleamarket in search of another, identical, pot at a bargain price.

The ultimate in Austrian collecting mania is exemplified by a museum dedicated to useless inventions and presided over by an Association for the Exploitation of Surplus Ideas. The exhibition hall is called a Nonseum, and although the comedy wears a bit thin after you've seen a few 'alternative lawn-mowers', pieces of 'diet crockery', 'heatable garden gnomes' and 'portable zebra crossings', the show's underlying affection for the tendency to redundancy in human endeavour reflects a widespread Austrian view.

> 66 The ultimate in Austrian collecting mania is exemplified by a museum dedicated to useless inventions. 99

Even as austere a figure as Sigmund Freud collected 'antiquities' on his visits to Italy and Greece, later transferring them to London when he had to flee Vienna. An exhibition of these knick-knacks was furnished with a catalogue containing a solemn exegesis of the relationship between Freud's ideas and his antiques.

> **Even as austere a figure as Sigmund Freud pedantically collected 'antiquities'.**

The Austrian's obsession with small, charming and useless objects has made him a shrewd judge of which parts of the Austrian heritage can best be marketed, and the souvenir industry offers foreign tourists several lines of shameless kitsch, which include figurines of Emperor Franz Joseph (*Kaiser-kitsch*), chocolates known as *Mozartkugeln* (i.e., Mozart balls) and even Klimt or Schiele T-shirts. In this way the Disneyland version of Austria past and present makes Austrians rich and foreigners happy.

Death

The Austrians' fascination with death also owes something to aristocratic tone-setting, notably the obsequies that made the death of an emperor something to look forward to. The spectacular aspect of funerals – what the Viennese call a *schöne Leich* (lovely corpse) – plays a vital role in their culture. This is because the

Austrians believe that death is a part of life, not simply the termination of it. 'He who would understand how a Viennese lives,' wrote Hermann Bahr, 'must know how he is buried: for his being is deeply bound up with his no-longer-being, about which he is constantly singing bitter-sweet songs.'

They say you can't take it with you, but Austrians seem at least to take their innumerable titles and honours with them. You

> **" The Austrians believe that death is a part of life, not simply the termination of it. "**

can see gravestones bearing the honorific inscriptions of innumerable doctors, *Meister* (for professionals and craftsmen, e.g., Master Baker, Master Plumber, Master Chimney Sweeper), not to mention *Hofrats*. All this may serve to remind the living of the forms of address expected of St. Peter when these distinguished persons arrive at the heavenly gates.

Rituals connected with death range from the picturesque to the macabre. In the former category is the custom whereby colleagues follow the bier of a former leading player at the Burgtheater as it makes a lap of honour round the theatre, before being despatched to the cemetery. In the macabre category is the gruesome necrolatry of the Habsburgs. For hundreds of years deceased emperors were carved up and distributed around the capital: hearts in one place, entrails in another and the rest in the Capuchin crypt.

Death-oriented attractions in Vienna include the

Burial Museum (in which the star item is a coffin with a bell-pull to alert passers-by should you happen to have been buried alive), and the vast Central Cemetery.

The project for a large central cemetery was first mooted in the 19th century by the city council, because the existing cemeteries were bursting at the seams. The thoroughness with which Austrians mull over everything concerning death and burial was immediately apparent in the ensuing deliberations.

Since the cemetery was to be far from the centre of town, and conservation of the corpses of the poor was not always all that it might have been, a certain Franz Felbinger proposed a mechanism for '*pneumatische Leichenbeförderung*' ('pneumatic transmission' of bodies – to the cemetery, that is, not to heaven). The corpses were to be lowered into a duct below a mortuary in central Vienna and then most satisfactorily and efficiently whooshed to the cemetery in a matter of minutes. Sadly this project failed to take off due to technical difficulties (there were worries that the corpses might get stuck half way along and begin to disintegrate before they could be extracted).

The Central Cemetery is a place of pilgrimage, especially on All Saints Day, when most of Vienna travels

> **The corpses were to be lowered into a duct below a mortuary then whooshed to the cemetery in a matter of minutes.**

out through the November mists to place a wreath on a family tomb or on the *Ehrengrab* (grave of honour) of some favourite actor or public figure. The cemetery is so large that the municipality runs a minibus to ferry the elderly along its silent avenues and employs a sharp-shooter who ventures out at dawn to shoot hares breakfasting on the succulent wreaths.

Suicide

A remarkably large number of Austrian intellectuals decide to pre-empt the decision of the Almighty. Some suicides seem eminently rational as responses to pro-tracted and fatal illness (such as those of the writers Adalbert Stifter, Ferdinand von Saar and Ludwig Hevesi); others were apparently the result of miscalcu-lation, like that of playwright Ferdinand Raimund, who erroneously thought he had contracted rabies after a dog-bite. In a quite different category was the case of the philosopher and self-styled genius Otto Weininger, who committed an attention-seeking sui-cide in the house where Beethoven died, whereas the physicist Ludwig Boltzmann, who really was a genius, ended his life as a consequence of depression and overwork.

Professor Ringel's strictures on Austrian parents are lent some support by the long list of suicides among the offspring and siblings of the famous. It includes two brothers of Austrian philosopher Wittgenstein, the sons of the physicist Ernst Mach and of the writer Hugo von Hofmannsthal, the daughter of Arthur Schnitzler and the brother of Gustav Mahler. There was also the architect Eduard van der Null who sank into terminal despair when the Emperor made a slighting remark about his opera house.

Another artist, Alfred Kubin, and the composers Alban Berg and Hugo Wolf all attempted suicide. Not to be outdone, the dynasty supplied the most spectacular suicide of all, when Crown Prince Rudolf shot his lover, Marie Vetsera, and then himself at Mayerling. Rudolf, who kept a skull on his desk as a *memento mori*, was simply one more in a long line of Austrians who opted for the short cut to the other side (although shooting his mistress at the same time was overstepping the conventions somewhat).

> **❝ A bonus for an Austrian of being safely dead is that his removal from the scene often brings the applause and recognition that was denied him in life. ❞**

Jumping off bridges over the Danube was such a regular occurrence in the 19th century that Vienna is one of the few places to have a burial place dedicated largely to suicides (*Friedhof der Namenlosen*, The Graveyard of the Nameless) which is situated downstream near Albern, at a spot where the corpses tended to wash up.

A bonus for an Austrian of being safely dead is that his removal from the scene often brings the applause and recognition that was denied him in life. Mortality is the pre-condition for immortality, or so it is often claimed, and Mozart is paraded as the 'awful example'. Mahler supplied a good aphorism to buttress the myth: *'Muss man denn in Österreich erst tot sein damit sie einen leben lassen?'* ('Have you actually got to be dead in Austria before they'll let you live?')

Leisure & Pleasure

Allotments

Austrian allotments (*Schrebergärten*) do not conform to the original concept which envisaged playground-parks for young people. Instead they were encouraged after the First World War so that people could grow their own vegetables in a time of shortage. Later they became the summer retreats (in true Austrian style hedged around not only by greenery, but also by innumerable rules and regulations) for the inhabitants of dank tenement houses on modest incomes.

> **"Austrian allotments are hedged around not only by greenery, but also by innumerable rules and regulations."**

The *Schrebergärten* of today are the last word in

Gemütlichkeit, each with a profusion of lovingly tended fruit trees and flowers, a pocket-handkerchief of lawn and a summer house. The younger generation now have more money than their elders did at their age and more free time to spend pursuing trendy sports like tennis, so *Schrebergärten* tend to be inhabited by the middle-aged and elderly. Many of these plots also boast a full complement of garden gnomes, indistinguishable in certain lights from their owners.

Mountain walking and hiking

Walking in the Alps and hiking in the Vienna Woods have long provided respite from his labour for the Austrian worker, and congenial relaxation for the middle-class. The rural pleasures of workers and burghers used to be rigorously marked off along the lines of a muffled *Kulturkampf* (clash

❝ Hiking is often conducted with an earnestness and dignity that brings to mind *The Happy Wanderer*. ❞

of cultures), which dictated the appropriate manner for enjoying them according to one's class allegiance.

Hiking is often conducted with an earnestness and dignity that brings to mind F.W. and E. Möller's 1954 worldwide hit, *The Happy Wanderer*, in particular the immortal lines: 'I raise my hat to all I meet, And they raise back to me', followed by a refrain of cautious ecstasy: 'Fal de rih, fal de rah, fal de ra ha ha ha, ra ha

48

ha ha, rah!'.

As far as the Viennese are concerned, a good day's rambling in the dark and gloomy Wienerwald is just what the doctor ordered, and can be combined with the ritualistic activity of mushroom hunting. In the late afternoon comes the climax of the day, a *Jause*, euphemistically described as a 'snack', but to non-Austrians a full meal of smoked sausage, cheese, bread, gherkins, etc.

The uniform for all this activity used to be the classic symbols of the great outdoors, Austrian-style, namely *Lederhosen* (leather breeches) and a dark felt hat with a thing like a shaving brush stuck in the hat-band. You did not have to be a mountaineer to wear it. Until recently it was possible to encounter a gentleman in full Alpine rig hurrying through a Vienna suburb with a purposeful air, setting out not for the mountains, but for an afternoon of sublime rusticity in his *Schrebergarten*.

> **66 As far as the Viennese are concerned, a good day's rambling in the dark and gloomy Wienerwald is just what the doctor ordered. 99**

Spectator sports

The most popular spectator sports are naturally those at which Austrians excel – winter sports and motor-racing. The former is to be expected but the latter is a bit of a puzzle. It is true that in the 19th century an

Austrian developed one of the first internal combustion engines and, like a number of other Austrian inventors, received little recognition and less thanks for doing so; but Niki Lauda is a phenomenon that has inspired a whole generation of Formula I aspirants.

Austria's winter sportsmen, especially skiers, are in a class of their own. You might think the Austrian sports commentators' endless recitation of their countrymen's names is exaggerated patriotism, until you realise that in most competitions several of the first ten places will have been won by Austrians.

> **Austria's winter sportsmen, especially skiers, are in a class of their own.**

As soon as some local hero has clipped a second off the slalom record or barely survived a death-defying ski-jump, a microphone is thrust in his face and he is invited to give his view of the matter. As this is usually delivered in impenetrable Tyrolean dialect, even German-speakers are little the wiser; however the translation usually turns out to be something along the lines of: 'I didn't think I could do it; but then I jumped; and then I did it!'

The career of a top-class ski-racer being somewhat short-lived, it is important to collect as many titles and give as many TV interviews as possible before retiring to open a hotel or to advertise washing powder.

Sex

The Austrians display for the most part a civilised and down-to-earth attitude to the physical side of affairs of the heart. Most quietly ignore the attitude of the Catholic Church to such matters as contraception and abortion (the latter being legal in Austria if carried out in the first three months of pregnancy). Prudery is lacking in the Austrian temperament and chastity is regarded as something only suitable for those who have chosen it.

Austrians are more relaxed about irregular liaisons than more judgmental northerners. The euphemisms for describing the participants lack the pruri-ence beloved of English puritans. A gallant who makes love to a married woman may be known as the *Hausfreund* (house friend) – an innuendo that often attaches to similar words such as *Freundin* (female friend); and unmarried people in steady relationships are each other's *Lebensgefährten* and *Lebensgefährtinnen* (life companions), terms which conjure up a pleasing image of bosom friends on the long road of life.

> **A gallant who makes love to a married woman may be known as the *Hausfreund* (house friend).**

An anecdote sums up the general attitude to irregu-lar sexual arrangements: Two men meet for the first time at a party. By way of conversation one says to the other, 'You see those two women chatting to each other in the corner? The brunette is my wife and the pretty blonde she's talking to is my mistress.' 'That's funny,' says the other man, 'I was just about to say the same thing, only the other way round.'

Culture

Austrian high culture was traditionally and not surprisingly centred on places where patronage was available (e.g. the Habsburg court in Vienna, or that of the Prince Archbishops of Salzburg). The church also played an important role, not least in educating musicians or giving them employment (Bruckner at the Monastery of Sankt Florian in Upper Austria,

66 There are cultural offerings nationwide, from gnat-infested open-air operettas to avant-garde festivals. 99

Haydn as a choirboy at St. Stephen's in Vienna). Since the (20th-century) founding of the modern Salzburg Festival by Max Reinhardt and its transformation by

von Karajan into an obligatory photo opportunity for the glitterati, Salzburg and Vienna have come to dominate cultural activity with events almost all the year round.

Today there are cultural offerings nationwide, from gnat-infested open-air operettas at tiny Mörbisch on the Neusiedler See in the east, to avant-garde festivals in Graz to the south, or mainstream to popular drama and opera during the summer at Bregenz in the west. However, when Austrian cultural achievements are considered, it is Vienna that springs to mind, for it is the city of composers – Haydn, Mozart, Schubert, Bruckner, Mahler, Schönberg and Johann Strauss (all sons of Austria or the Habsburg Empire), and of German composers Beethoven and Brahms who largely made their careers in Vienna and died there; of artists – Klimt and the Vienna Secession; of writers – Raimund, Grillparzer, Nestroy, Kraus; of dramatists – von Hofmannsthal, Schnitzler; and

> **The streets of Vienna are surfaced with culture, those of other cities with asphalt.**

of Sigmund Freud; the birthplace of Friedrich von Hayek, Karl Popper and Ernst Gombrich. Many of these are universal geniuses and it can be argued that there is nothing especially or uniquely Austrian about them. Yet the quality and multiplicity of their achievements suggest at the very least that Vienna provided an environment in which creativity flourished: as Kraus sardonically remarked, 'The streets of Vienna are surfaced with culture, those of other cities with asphalt.'

What a performance

A feature of the Austrian passion for culture which is at its most formidable in Vienna and replicated on a

provincial scale throughout Austria, is extreme parti-
sanship. Feuding over artistic matters is something
that comes as naturally to the Austrians as breathing.
Passions of unbelievable ferocity are displayed for and
against new opera productions, or for and against a
contemporary playwright's
latest kick in the national
groin. It was ever so: in the
19th century music lovers
were divided into a Wagnerian
faction, which supported
Bruckner, and a traditional faction supporting
Brahms. The latter's music has been described as
'exactly suited to Viennese tastes – not too hot and
not too cold', making it sound like a lukewarm bath.

**66 Feuding over
artistic matters is
something that comes as
naturally to the Austrians
as breathing. 99**

While culture certainly provides an excellent excuse
for quarrelling, itself an art form in Austria and one
that has been developed to a high degree of sophisti-
cation, Austrians do care deeply about music, art and
theatre.

An object of veneration is the Vienna Philharmonic,
founded in 1842. The orchestra formerly constituted a
priestly caste from which women were rigorously
excluded. However, arguments such as the one that
women 'lack a muscle in the upper arm essential to a
supreme vibrato' are wearing thin, and the
Philharmoniker is slowly being forced to change its
entrance criteria. Now the odd lady violinist may be

seen among the serried ranks of male Philharmoniker if you study the TV screen closely when their famous New Year's Day Concert is broadcast.

Its members (still for the most part native Viennese) receive generous salaries by musicians' standards, which are topped up by a steady of royalties from best-selling CDs. Subscribers' tickets (theoretically the only ones available) to the Philharmonic's Sunday morning concerts are passed down in families from generation to generation and attendance is a social as well as a musical ritual.

The theatre, too, has been described as 'a necessity of life for the Austrians that takes second place only to eating and drinking'. Indeed it has often been diffi-cult to know where life on the stage ends and life on the street begins. Since Baroque times theatre and opera have flourished in Vienna, the public's taste for mega-shows

> **66 The theatre has been described as 'a necessity of life for the Austrians that takes second place only to eating and drinking'. 99**

being as insatiable as it could be undiscriminating. Maria Theresa decreed that 'there must be spectacles' to keep the hoi polloi amused and Adolf Hitler played to a full house when delivering his hour-long rant on the Heldenplatz in 1938. (Like many Austrians, he was himself a frustrated artist, the cultural glories of Vienna inspiring in him a mixture of admiration, hatred and envy.)

The dramatist Grillparzer has evoked that sense of the frustrated artist which lies just under the skin of many an Austrian and finds expression in everything from DIY skills to virtuosity on the violin: 'One lives in half-poetry, dangerous to whole art, and is a poet though one never dreamt of rhyme or stanza.'

Home entertainment

Couch-potato culture has not yet attained the dominance in Austria that it exercises elsewhere. This may be because the high quality of Austrian television acts as a deterrent to mass viewing, although in the hope of wooing younger viewers, 'reality shows'

> **66 The high quality of Austrian television acts as a deterrent to mass viewing. 99**

and versions of *Who Wants to Be a Millionaire?* have seeped into the schedules.

Less affected is the radio, with several serious discussion programmes and an abundance of music, although listeners complain that too much of the latter is 'modern' (that is to say not *Wiener Klassik*, Strauss, and so forth). This might come as a surprise to visitors, who have an impression of wall-to-wall Mozart, even on the answering services of the offices they try to ring. Public toilets in the underpass by the Oper play loud Strauss waltzes that compete with the swishes and sighs of the urinals and WCs. However, disgruntled listeners can turn to the church-supported Radio Stephansdom, whose musical fare is reassuringly traditional – something Austrians wake up to, enjoy during their lunch hour and use as the most agreeable of sleeping pills – quartets on the quarter hour, masses for the masses.

Government & Bureaucracy

Party politics

Three main parties bestraddle the Austrian political scene: the Austrian Social Democratic Party (SPÖ), known as the 'Reds', the Austrian People's Party (ÖVP – Conservatives) known as the 'Blacks', and the fissiparous right-wing Freedom Party of Austria (FPÖ), whose colour is blue, but whose more extreme adherents are referred to (and not flatteringly) as 'brown'. (This is a reference to the

66 All Austrians are keen to have reform, just as long as everything stays the same. 99

favoured brown of Nazi uniforms.) There is also an influential Green Party, whose colour is ...well ... green.

The entry of the 'Blues' in 2000 into the government marked a sea-change in Austrian politics and society. This followed years of largely cosmetic changes, in which, as one of the 'Black' ministers sardonically put it, 'All Austrians are keen to have reform, just as long as everything stays the same.' Because avoidance of risk is a key element in the national psyche, evading conflict had become the central plank of national (and personal) strategies for survival. A remarkably sophisticated aspect of this was the 'Social Partnership', an unofficial arrangement by which political stability (or stasis, according to your point of view) had been secured since its institution in 1957. Crucial decisions on wages and prices were agreed by a commission which officially had no legal standing, and were then endorsed by the Conservative interest (e.g. the Chambers of Commerce and Agriculture) and its Socialist counterparts (e.g. the Chamber of Labour and the Trades Unions).

> 66 The system was typically Austrian in that all its advantages could be described as disadvantages, and vice versa. 99

The results were impressive – years of steady growth and low unemployment, with time lost in strikes famously counted in seconds per year. However the system was also typically Austrian in that all its advantages could be described as disadvantages, and vice versa. Thus the benefits of the political stability produced by the long-term coalition of 'Reds' and 'Blacks' led to (non-existent) jobs for the boys, multiple salaries and much else that the then leader of the Blues, Jörg Haider, hastened to bring to the attention of the Austrian voters.

Like the Austrian church, social democracy is in danger of sinking under the weight of its own anachronistic baggage.

Bureaucracy

Austrians are used to being burdened with thousands of petty restrictions, and one of the main preoccupations of any self-respecting citizen is to find ways of evading those he finds uncongenial. To avoid bureaucratic obstructions, *Hintertürln* (back doors) are used, the exploitation of which requires years of practice. However, those responsible for enforcing regulations may also adopt a cavalier attitude towards them,

> **66** One of the main preoccupations of any self-respecting citizen is to find ways of evading petty restrictions he finds uncongenial. **99**

depending upon such imponderables as the state of the policeman's digestion and whether or not the dreaded *Föhn* (south wind) is blowing.

The delicately poised ambivalence of the official mind is deftly evoked by Austrian cultural critic Jörge Mauthe in his description of a typical ministry building, characterised by many long corridors. At the end of one of these is a permanently closed door bearing the legend, 'Entry for all persons is strictly forbidden.'

'Since a door by its very nature would seem to embody the idea, indeed predicate the possibility of access,' writes Mauthe, 'to find such an instruction posted on one is more than a little odd. Even odder, however, is the injunction beneath this all-embracing prohibition, namely: *Mind the step*.'

Austrian bureaucracy is a work of art, and bureaucratic procedure pursues its own remorseless logic to sometimes surreal conclusions. It is not surprising that senior Austrian bureaucrats have often been aesthetes or writers like Stifter or Grillparzer, men who combined absolute loyalty in the sphere of duty with restrained opposition in the sphere of art. Many of them had a creditable record of disinterested administration under the Habsburgs, when the bureaucracy and the army supplied the glue for holding together diverse races and traditions.

> **❝ Austrian bureaucracy is a work of art, and bureaucratic procedure pursues its own remorseless logic to sometimes surreal conclusions. ❞**

Despite this, bureaucracy is something with which the Austrian has a love-hate relationship (actually *Hassliebe* – the hate comes first in German). One part of him hates its nagging interference in the remotest corners of his affairs, while another part of him does not want to see the end of the halcyon realms of *Verwaltung* (state administration), where you cannot be sacked once you are *pragmatisiert* (on the permanent staff) and days of tenured pen-pushing are rewarded with the inflated pension that such a stressful career naturally commands.

In the 19th century bureaucrats retired to the sunny climes of Graz, which was known less than respectfully as *Pensionopolis*. Today the pensioned official is to be recognised by a permanent tan acquired on several package tours a year.

Individual *Beamten* (officials) can be diligent, charming, courteous and possessed of a high degree of self-irony in the Austrian way. On the other

> **The pensioned official is to be recognised by a permanent tan acquired on several package tours a year.**

hand a grumpy official can be a formidable burden on reason and humanity. It is little consolation to discover that his or her obduracy may simply be due to tactical manoeuvring in some obscure and ever-ongoing departmental squabble. The most famous such example was when a Hungarian was appointed Director of the Austrian Museum of Modern Art. Some six months after his appointment, he was startled to receive a communication from the Aliens Bureau instructing him to leave the country 'forthwith'. Despite his perfectly legal appointment by the Ministry of Science, treasury officials opposed to it had managed to sit on his contract so long that he had technically become an illegal resident.

Less elevated mortals can seek and get redress for bureaucratic blunders through the *Volksanwalt* (People's Lawyer) – an institution whose activities show that constraints on misuse of executive power are taken much more seriously in Austria than elsewhere. The importance of such constraints was underlined by a statement from the head of the Law Society, in which he complained that Austria is in danger of being 'administered to death', such is the hail of laws, amendments and extensions thereto falling daily upon the heads of the population.

> **Austria is in danger of being 'administered to death', such is the hail of laws, amendments and extensions thereto.**

For this, of course, the official cannot be held responsible, but it is a situation that naturally gives him a daunting measure of power. A line in the national anthem runs '*vielgeprüftes Österreich*' (much-tried Austria). *Prüfen* also means 'to examine' and the satirists have recast the final two verses: 'Much-examined Austria (In respect of the Revenue); Much-examined Austria (In respect of the National Audit Office).' You may think you will get away with something, but some bureaucrat with *Sitzfleisch* (diligence) in some inconspicuous little office behind a door marked 'Entry Forbidden' is on your trail...

Systems

The collapse of Empire in 1918, followed by occupation and total war, meant that in 1945 Austria went back to the drawing board. The Marshall Plan, and the achievement of neutral independence after the State Treaty of 1955, released a flood of resources for reconstruction and modernisation. The Austrians had the talent, were given the money, and modern Austria is the result.

The way in which they did it reflects the Austrian genius for mixing the old with the new, as also for aestheticising technology. The latter is, of course, expected to function smoothly and usually does; but it is also required to conform to the ever important national requirement of *Gemütlichkeit*.

> **" State-of-the-art computers are tastefully arranged in restored palaces as though the original architect had envisaged them there. "**

State-of-the-art computers are tastefully arranged in restored palaces as though the original architect had envisaged them there; passengers emerge from an ultra-modern U-Bahn through a whimsical Secessionist pavilion. The marriage of tradition with modernity is a remarkably happy one: the spotless and noiseless metro glides under the ancient inner city of Vienna, sharing its subterranean secrets with Romanesque remains and medieval cellars; trams (relegated to the scrap heap of history by other, less prudent nations) negotiate the streets of Vienna and Graz at an average speed of ten miles an hour, but this is lightning-like progress compared with the daily snarl-ups in London, Paris or Rome.

Austrians are as ambivalent about modernity as they are about everything else, and especially enjoy the verbal demolition of what they take to be megalo-mania on the part of architects. Happily for the critics, there has always been a steady supply of projects which combine massive outlay with spectacular uselessness. 'For hare-brained schemes and stupidities,' wrote one commentator, 'there is always plenty of money in Austria. What prestige is there in a project that is merely sensible?'

> 66 'For hare-brained schemes and stupidities, there is always plenty of money in Austria. What prestige is there in a project that is merely sensible?' 99

Meanwhile, the infrastructure is kept going by a continuous flow of investment in public works. The only drawback is that almost every institution, museum, autobahn, etc., appears to be in a more or less permanent state of *Umbau* (rebuilding). Conversations with minor officials, booking clerks and hall porters always seem to be conducted in competition with a pneumatic drill. Notices mushroom bearing legends such as 'Closed on account of building works. We hope you will understand', or 'Transferred to number 14, such and such street, due to renovation works'; or, more ominously, 'Closed for the time being'.

Education

The Austrians have a reverence for *Bildung*, a term that implies the possession of culture as well as mere knowledge. Some of the most brilliant minds of the 20th century were nurtured in the hothouse atmosphere of the Vienna *Gymnasien* (selective secondary schools).

There are nine years of compulsory schooling in Austria and though the church-run schools still have some segregated classes all state school classes are co-educational. At ten, pupils divide into two streams, one vocationally oriented and one leading to the secondary school diploma known as the *Matura*.

> **❝ The Austrians have a reverence for *Bildung*, a term that implies the possession of culture as well as mere knowledge. ❞**

Armed with the latter you have the right to be admitted to university, provided you can pay the fees that have been introduced to reduce overcrowding, high drop-out rates during the first year, the phenomenon of the 'eternal student' and the glut of over-qualified people in the jobs market, factors that seriously undermine Austria's justifiably high reputation in further education.

The average duration of study in Austria is seven years, the European average being four and a half. At the faculty of medicine, the mills grind so slowly that students generally require ten years to reach the finishing line: having got there, they discover that the powerful 'Chamber of Doctors' operates a job cartel, whereby they control the number of doctors admitted to practise. Naturally the Chamber protests that this is solely to protect the public interest. Equally naturally the public in whose interest they are so assiduous (and who recall the hours spent in doctors' waiting rooms) do not believe them.

> **66 The idea of making army discipline in some way _gemütlich_ (cosy) is charmingly Austrian. 99**

Young Austrians are required to do a stint of national service or equivalent community service. Since more and more opt for community service, the authorities are casting around in some desperation to make military service more 'attractive'. (The idea of making army discipline in some way _gemütlich_ (cosy) is charmingly Austrian, but seems unlikely to catch on.)

Environment

Austria is in the forefront of environmental protection by European standards. Indeed, an absurd situation arose whereby the E.U. wanted some of Austria's standards to be lowered to accommodate businesses in countries which operate under more lax E.U. rules. This did not go down well in Austria. People-power had already forced the government to mothball a nuclear power station at astronomic cost and to abandon plans to build a hydro-electric dam on the Danube.

In domestic politics the government has got pro-gressively greener, banning leaded petrol, issuing ordinances for the separation of waste for recycling, and even forcing indignant lighting shops to take back expired fluorescent tubes.

Eating & Drinking

The food habits of the Austrians have been dictated for a very long time by quantity rather than quality. The names for many traditional dishes are redolent of quivering mounds of food exploding on the palate like the cholesterol bombs they so often describe. *Bauernschmaus*, for instance, means 'peasants' treat' and consists of a great heap of meats and sausages only a little smaller than the Grossglockner (Austria's highest mountain), garnished with dumplings and sauerkraut. Macho eaters can test their staying power on *Beuschel* (chopped offal in sauce) or *Blunzn* (black pudding).

Inevitably, some middle-aged Austrians bear a striking resemblance to popular items on the national menu such as *Fleischknödeln* (potato dumplings filled with meat) and *Grammelknödeln* (more dumplings, only stuffed with pork scratchings).

Boiled beef is a favourite dish (cooked by the purists for four hours), yet it has never achieved the universal approbation enjoyed by that other speciality, the *Wiener Schnitzel*. A decent *Wiener Schnitzel*, say the cognoscenti, should be 'the size of a lavatory seat' (*abortdeckelgross*) and, just as with lavatory seats, it is frowned upon to share one between two. The real thing, dipped in egg and breadcrumbs, fried in butter until golden brown, and seasoned with lemon is, in itself, worth the journey to Vienna.

> **A decent *Wiener Schnitzel*, say the cognoscenti, should be 'the size of a lavatory seat'.**

Cake, bake and take

Vienna shares with Salzburg (and indeed virtually any Austrian town worthy of the name) a *Konditorei* (cake shop) tradition that would fulfil one's wildest dreams.

All over Austria ladies of a certain age and girth gravitate in the mid-afternoon to the nearest cake shop. The choice before them is bewilderingly large – a dazzling range of cakes with the names of the chefs who invented them or the aristocrats who consumed them (Sacher, Esterhazy, Malakoff, Dobos); there are sponge slices garnished with blackberries, bilberries, raspberries or strawberries; not to mention the petits fours, chocolate fingers and strawberry tarts. The *Konditorei* is primarily a female haunt, a place where ladies who have accepted defeat in the battle of the bulge can sink comfortably into late middle age like ships sliding slowly beneath the waves.

Bakeries have an astonishing range of wheat or rye loaves, many of them seasoned with cumin. The latter is valuable as a carminative, which explains the intestinal winds approaching gale force that often follow the consumption of Austrian bread. Bakeries also offer brioches, croissants, filled rolls and numerous pastries. For those who want to devour their purchases on the spot with a cup of coffee, there is usually a counter

> **66 All over Austria ladies of a certain age and girth gravitate in the mid-afternoon to the nearest cake shop. 99**

along the back wall. This facility is much used by the ubiquitous Viennese *Plaudertaschen* (gossipy windbags) airing a few scandals as they scoff their *Plundertaschen* – puff pastries filled with plum jam.

Urban Austrians appear to need gastronomic support even for the merest walk to the post office or the newspaper stand: how else can you account for the fact that every few yards you are assailed by good smells from a confectioner or bakery, a doughnut stand, a sandwich shop, a butcher's shop with its own eating counter or a *Würstelstand* (street corner booth).

The latter are placed in strategic proximity to public transport junctions and offer a variety of hot sausages such as fat-squirting *Debreziners* and *Burenwurst*, or *Käsekrainer*, a sausage known as *eitrige* (meaning 'pus-filled') because when you bite into it the cheese filling oozes out. The gherkins, mustard and roll that accompany these delicacies represent a largely futile attempt to break down or mop up the fat content. The least enticing substance on offer from the *Würstelständ* is *Leberkäse* or meat-loaf which has a faintly disturbing pink complexion, turning slowly to grey when in terminal decline. It sits in its glass oven on the counter, sweating slightly and giving off a pungent odour, as if defying you to eat it.

66 It is doubtful whether the real Austrian trencherman would be greatly impressed by food that might prolong life and keep the waistline in check. 99

The attractions of cheap food in cities pullulating with tempting but expensive gastronomic offerings are obvious enough; and even if price were not a consideration, it is doubtful whether the real Austrian trencherman would be greatly impressed by food that might prolong life and keep the waistline in check. He prefers to contemplate, with admirable stoicism, the not entirely disagreeable prospect of '*Selbstmord mit Messer und Gabel*' ('suicide with a knife and fork').

The Kaffeehaus

The Kaffeehaus has always played a special role in Viennese culture, with provincial imitations in the university towns. It has been described as 'a place for people who want to be alone, but who need society to achieve this'. Choosing a coffee-house is an exercise in discrimination. There are dingy ones where rather rough-looking people play billiards, and shabby, genteel ones where garrulous pensioners play bridge. One may be full of *Beamten* who carefully add up the bill instead of just paying it; another is populated by intellectuals reading the newspapers which are provided free.

> **❝ The Kaffeehaus has been described as 'a place for people who want to be alone, but who need society to achieve this'. ❞**

The coffee house is useful for filling in those gaps in the day when there is nothing pressing to do. Naturally the older you are, the more substantial these are likely to be. It was said of one elderly couple: 'For ten years the two of them sat for hours each day quite alone in a coffee house. 'That is a good marriage!' you will say. No, that's a good coffee house.'

Drinking

The Austrians' enthusiasm for indifferent beer is as nothing when compared to their passion for fizzy young wine. In wine-growing areas the local inns are known as *Heurigen*. The name comes from the word

> **The thoughts of many, when in their cups, soon turn to depression and death.**

heuer meaning 'this year', and indicates that only young wine from the previous harvest and from a single vineyard can be offered. Atmosphere and tradition are what distinguish the *Heurige*, being just as important as the quality of the (mostly white) wine, which many prefer to drink *gespritzt* (splashed with soda or mineral water).

The quality most associated with drinking is *Gemütlichkeit*, which in this context implies informality, conviviality and cosiness. Geniality usually takes a form that is bewildering to those not fully attuned to the vagaries of the Austrian character, for the thoughts of many, when in their cups, soon turn to depression and death.

The undertow of melancholy, for which the wine is no doubt responsible in more ways than one, undercuts the unrestrained sentimentality and gives *Heurige* drinking sessions a macabre spice like a drop of urine in a cup of nectar. A modern troubadour, Roland Neuwirth, has satirized this tendency in his *Genuine Viennese Song* which offers 15 metaphors for dying.

These include: 'to lay aside your slippers', 'to hand in your spoon', 'to begin to view the potatoes from underneath', and 'to put on wooden pyjamas'.

Shopping

In Austria the actual business of shopping is subject to unwritten codes that the shopper ignores at his peril. In supermarkets the model shopper indicates his intent to buy when he collects a wire basket or trolley at the entrance. All Austrians dutifully do this so they cannot be accused of slipping things into their pockets as they go round. Approaching the checkout, customers are confronted by large notices stating that personal shopping bags should be held up for inspection 'to avoid misunderstandings'.

Much more congenial than the big stores are the little men of Austrian retailing – stall-holders, lottery ticket vendors, 'Tabak' proprietors who sell tickets for public transport as well as newspapers and tobacco, and, last but not least, the *Greißler*. The latter are a Viennese phenomenon, corner-shop grocers who are said to be always on the verge of extinction due to supermarket competition (but who have been on the

❝Customers are confronted by large notices stating that personal shopping bags should be held up for inspection 'to avoid misunderstandings'.❞

verge for at least 30 years). *Greißler* have been described as 'selling everything from gherkins to homespun philosophy'. The substantial amount of the latter being transacted means they are often full of pensioners chattering like starlings. The shrewd owners remain studiously neutral on the burning issues of the day to safeguard their customers' continued patronage.

The Tabaks and lottery shops also attract their regulars, who like to linger over a cigarette while offering their captive audience a beguiling mixture of provincial wit and wisdom. Whenever a public scandal hits the headlines, it is hardly possible to get in, so great is the press of persons wishing to air an opinion.

> **❝ Tabaks and lottery shops also attract their regulars, who like to linger while offering a beguiling mixture of provincial wit and wisdom. ❞**

Austrian conservatism used to dictate that shopping hours accorded with the convenience of shopkeepers, rather than the shoppers. After some 30 years of wrangling between the relevant ministry and the more commercially attuned shopkeepers, shops mostly trade whenever they want between 0.00 hours on Monday and 17.00 hours on Saturday. You might think that the right to open your shop more or less when you see fit would not be contentious, but people who assume this fail to understand the mentality of the traditional Austrian shopkeeper. If he himself does not want to open at a particular time, then of course he wants a law preventing anyone else from doing so.

Suburban bank branches and a few post-offices in the country still close for one or even two hours over lunch-time, though this is precisely the time when most working people need to use such services. Austrians are understanding about this: lunch, after all, is a serious matter, and making money should not be allowed to take precedence over the workings of the digestion.

Health

The Austrians' interest in health is scientific, or at least pseudo-scientific. Health conversations are sprinkled with impressive terminology, and friendship requires that you listen to a blow-by-blow account of your friends' symptoms, then reciprocate with an exhaustive account of your own.

Diagnosis suits the Austrian temperament, indeed the enormous and well-earned reputation of the Viennese

❝ Diagnosis suits the Austrian temperament, indeed the enormous reputation of the Viennese Medical School was founded on it. ❞

Medical School was founded on it. Some 19th-century doctors took this to extremes: 'I diagnose that you need more diagnosis.' A German visitor in 1847 wrote a satirical poem describing learned Viennese professors energetically taking notes as the patient deteriorated before their eyes and finally expired. Death, of course, provided the opportunity for postmortem examination, followed by more diagnostic discussion.

Centres of health

Austrian medical treatment is provided through a system of mandatory insurance administered by 'Sickness Funds'. These operate out of fabulous glass and marble palaces, their executive layers traditionally packed with the recipients of political patronage. Top management draws the vast salaries customary on such Austrian gravy trains and the government picks up the bill for the funds' deficits.

> **66 A satirical poem described learned Viennese professors energetically taking notes as the patient deteriorated before their eyes. 99**

The system actually works well, probably because most of its funding is direct. Problems only arise when mistakes or scandals occur, at which point, following a well-established ritual, responsibility is passed round the multiplicity of bodies which have a finger in the health system pie: the Hospital Authority, the Provincial Government, the Federal Ministry for Health, the Federal Ministry for Education, Science and Culture, etc. Each of these in turn inspects the responsibility with an air of bewilderment and disgust, before announcing that it does not really belong in its sphere of competence, and passing it on.

Dietary health

Austrian males of the new generation are more fitness- and diet-conscious than their forebears. They are therefore less likely to degenerate into incipient heart attacks on two fat legs. The shambling, pot-bellied *Wurstfresser* (sausage gobblers) are dying out, although they always live longer than they or their doctors predict. It has yet to be seen whether the new Austrian with his vegetarian and mineral water tendencies keeps up that regimen beyond the age of 40.

Business

Austria's monopolistic and corporative approaches to business have often been evident, although such attitudes are now increasingly under attack and the trend to more competition has gathered momentum.

Despite, or perhaps because of, restrictive practices, Austria's economy has long been one of the wonders of the post-war world. Growth has been remarkably sustained and the country appeared miraculously immune to the worst effects of the recessions that smote other countries. A rare faltering of nation's economy in the early 1990s had the effect of highlighting the parlous state of the country's conglomerate state industries, which had finally imploded after years of slack management and (in some cases) corruption. Business and politics in Austria do not always operate in healthy symbiosis. As the state consortia were broken up and offered for privatisation, Austrians fondly hoped that such collusion would become less frequent in future.

> **66 Business and politics in Austria do not always operate in healthy symbiosis. 99**

The most spectacular privatisation was that of Austria Telekom, the removal of whose monopoly meant a reduction in tariffs of up to 30%. The Post Office is taking no chances. In a bid to keep the public on side, local branches embark on sporadic charm offensives. Counter clerks astound customers by no longer barking instructions at them or glowering at their packages. Campaigns include post boxes suddenly sporting messages of joy and welcome. Only a truly cold-hearted wretch could pass by a mail-box stickered with the words: '*Ich fühle mich so leer!*' ('I feel so empty!') without putting something in it.

Throughout the cold war the country benefited from deals with the East Bloc so that, when the Iron Curtain fell, Austrian businessmen had excellent contacts in many former Communist countries and moved in with great skill to exploit the best opportunities. The good news is that trade with Eastern Europe has grown. The less good news is that former Communist states can undercut Austrian business costs in many areas, due to their pools of skilled but cheap labour. However Austrian firms have profited from this by moving production to these neighbouring countries, investing heavily in joint ventures and businesses such as Hungarian breweries, as well as setting up branches of banks.

❝ Scepticism about the motives of businessmen is deeply ingrained in the attitudes of the ordinary Austrian. ❞

Nonetheless scepticism about the motives of businessmen is deeply ingrained in the attitudes of the ordinary Austrian. This is not surprising given the secretive manner in which executives love to operate. As late as 2000, a major supermarket chain was brazenly refusing to publish full accounts on the grounds of 'business confidentiality'.

Supervisory boards (Austria's equivalent of non-executives) can be kept totally in the dark about what the main board is up to – or sometimes vice versa. When the announcement was made that two of Austria's biggest banks were planning to merge, the puzzled Chief Executive of one of them complained to reporters that the first he knew about the imminent merger was when the news media reported it.

Crime & Punishment

Scandal

In the daily press scandals range from abuse of expenses (expenses are a way of life in Austria) to tax evasion and illicit arms deals. One involving massive corruption in the building of a new General Hospital for Vienna dragged on for more than a decade, and another involving a cartel of contractors tendering for infrastructure projects ran almost as long. The perpetrators have a Houdini-like propensity for escaping from tight corners. The few who are convicted quite often get off with a fine and a gentle rap over the knuckles, leaving the court with an air of injured merit, as if the whole thing had been some ghastly misunderstanding.

> **❝ In the daily press scandals range from abuse of expenses (expenses are a way of life in Austria) to tax evasion. ❞**

Schmäh

Austrians are fascinated by, and half in love with, those who pull off deceptions that leave the police, psychiatrists, politicians and indeed anyone in authority looking foolish. The man who stole the priceless Cellini salt-cellar from Vienna's Kunsthistorisches Museum, and led the police to where it was buried some years later, was one such.

Particularly stylish deception is known as *Schmäh* (a word peculiar to Austria), and the feats of its practitioners are recorded with enormous glee: few could resist the exploits of 'Auntie Hermine' who walked out of Austria with millions in her battered suitcase as a runner for corrupt building contractors. Then there were the big names associated with a food chain swindle, a scam of such stunning simplicity that

> 66 Particularly stylish deception is known as *Schmäh*, and the feats of its practitioners are recorded with enormous glee. 99

one wonders why no-one had thought of it before. As soon as the expiry date on packaged meat had come round, the products were removed from the shelves, conscientiously restamped with a new expiry date and returned to display.

The undisputed master of *Schmäh* was a criminal named Udo Proksch, an insurance swindler, who used to entertain politicians of all shades (but primarily Socialists) in a private room of the famous Viennese coffee-house of Demel, which he owned. These contacts stood him in good stead when he became a prime suspect in an insurance scam involving the sinking of a cargo ship with loss of life. After a few years on the run he became homesick for the fleshpots of Vienna and tried to slip back to Austria in disguise. To the embarrassment of certain highly placed persons, the British authorities at Heathrow were tactless enough to tip off their Austrian counterparts and there was no alternative but to arrest Proksch as he came through immigration. Thus ended a remarkable exercise in slow-motion detection reminiscent of a flight and pursuit nightmare, but one in which it is the pursuer whose legs never seem to carry him forward.

Language

Proverbial sayings in Austria reflect ambivalent attitudes to history and to national character. Those that have passed into the language typically recall blunders or faux pas, especially of the executive branch. The most famous is *'Alles gerettet, Majestät'* ('Everyone's safe, your Majesty'), the over-anxious-to-please report of the police chief to Franz Joseph after the Ringtheater had burned down in 1881. (In fact, 386 people had been incinerated.)

> 66 Many expressions recall the Austrians dislike of interlopers who tried to impose their outlandish ways on him. 99

Many expressions recall the Austrian's dislike of interlopers who tried to impose their outlandish ways on him. The phrases 'To make a Spanish face' and 'It's all Spanish to me' analogous to 'It's all Greek to me' date from the time when the Austrian Habsburgs imported a gloomy and unpleasant Spanish retinue, which insisted on sterile and rigid etiquette.

There is an abundance of words and phrases designed to bring down the officious or the vain a peg or two; an *Adabei*, for instance, is one who must always be *dabei*, i.e. present and seen to be present, at every fun ction. Similar meanings are attached to *Gschaftlhuber* – Chief of the Fire Brigade, President of the

> 66 There is an abundance of words and phrases designed to bring down the officious or the vain a peg or two. 99

Ten-Pin Bowling Club, Treasurer of the Glee Club, Lieutenant in the Salvation Army, etc., all rolled into one. Officiousness is also castigated in the delectable phrase *'Schnittling auf allen Suppen'* (a chive on every soup).

Even *Beamtensprache* (officialese) can be captivating, for who could resist *das lebende Inventar* (livestock) to describe the teaching staff in an elite school? Or the self-mocking *Löschmeister* (extinguishing master) to describe a Fire Superintendent? Other words derive their effect from their musical or onomatopoeic qualities – it comes as no surprise to learn that *Schnorrer* and *Schmarotzer* both mean 'sponger', while *Kerzlschlucker* (candle-cormorant) is an insufferably pious person who never misses a mass.

Sometimes the concept behind it is more entertaining than the sound of a word: the Austrians' equivalent of a beer belly, for example, is known as a *Backhendlfriedhof* – cemetery for fried chickens.

The trendy second language of the upwardly mobile is English, which has steadily penetrated the realms of fashion, business and politics. Words like 'super', 'fit' and 'clever' abound in everyday speech, as do phrases like 'sorry' (usually ironic in Austrian usage, implying no remorse whatever).

In Austria the worn or mundane phrase is always being given a new spin or a subtly nuanced intonation that makes the apparently innocent lethal, and the lethal sound innocent. In the hands of a master the language is constantly reframed to produce a stream of freshly minted expressions. But an Austrian, being an Austrian, hardly expects his genius in this or any other regard to be recognised as it deserves. He therefore turns even his neglect into an aphorism, like Grillparzer, who

> **66 The Austrians' equivalent of a beer belly is known as a *Backhendlfriedhof* – cemetery for fried chickens. 99**

grumbled: 'You won't get any recognition in this neck of the woods. In Austria they don't hang [the Order of] the Golden Cross on genius; but they'll sure as hell hang a genius on the cross...'

Conversation & Gestures

Austrians possess such an armoury of subtly insulting verbal weapons that they do not need to wave their arms about to make a point. Indeed, to outward appearances they are a phlegmatic lot. It is not unusual to see a guest at a party sitting in thoughtful silence throughout the evening, no doubt following Wittgenstein's useful precept: 'Whereof one cannot speak, thereof must one be silent.'

Austrians indeed have an almost infinite capacity for being unimpressed by verbal claims and boasting, the coun-

> **66** Austrians have an almost infinite capacity for being unimpressed by verbal claims and boasting. **99**

terpart of being rather easily impressed by spectacles. Frequently heard is the dismissive comment, *'Er macht sich wichtig'* ('He's trying to make himself important'), and the *Wichtigtuerei* (pomposity) of know-alls meets with a healthy degree of scorn.

If arrogance or deviousness needs to be exposed, local prejudice is often pressed into service. In particular, people in the provinces have a somewhat jaundiced view of the Viennese character which they express in such terms as a *'wiendiger Typ'* – a shady character; or the assertion: *'Wer nichts wird, wird Wiener'* – 'Anybody who wants to be a nobody becomes a Viennese'. The Viennese reciprocate in kind with slighting references to 'Tyrolean dumplings' or 'East Frisians', the latter a lethal description for the people of Burgenland, who have thus (quite unfairly) become a byword for irremediable stupidity.

Grumbling and whingeing are staples of Austrian, conversation. 'Not to let an Austrian criticize is to castrate him,' claims the sex counsellor, Gerti Senger. It is combined, however, with a great deal of personal charm and courtesy and an outsider might be inclined to think of it as aggression wrapped in obsequiousness.

The more refined forms of grumbling are transmuted into philosophical pessimism, the Austrian's talent for which is part and parcel of his faculty for self-diagnosis. A vivid description of professional gloom is provided by the futurologist Professor Millendorfer, who once remarked that the outlook for Austria in 20 or 50 years was good, provided the nation managed to survive the next five. However, one day he seemed to be looking (for him) remarkably cheerful. Asked why, he explained, 'Things are getting better for us.' 'I am pleased to hear that,' replied his colleague. 'Are the suicide statistics perhaps on the decline?' 'No,' said Professor Millendorfer, 'They remain strikingly constant. But everywhere else in the world they are showing a huge rise.'

66 **'Not to let an Austrian criticize is to castrate him,' claims the sex counsellor, Gerti Senger.** 99

The Author

Louis James has spent some 25 more or less fruitful years in contemplation of *Homo austriacus*. Despite being in daily contact with the species, he suspects that it is easier to describe the yeti (on which there is no verifiable information), than the Austrian (on which there is far too much, all of it contradictory). Notwithstanding this difficulty he has conducted many hours of diligent field work in cafés, wine-cellars, etc., refining his impressions for the present study, and was gratified to discover that many Austrian friends and acquaintances were prepared to assist selflessly with this.

Since settling in Vienna he has written regular reports on the Central European enigma, chiefly in the hope that sooner or later he will discover a new key to it (the old one having been thrown into the Danube some time ago). If, as seems likely, his efforts in this regard are crowned with failure, he anticipates that few will notice the fact but he will be considerably more popular with those who do.

The French

Intellectually and spiritually the French still associate themselves very much with the land, romanticising rural and village life to wild improbabilities. Inside every Bordeaux technocrat or sophisticated Parisian beats the heart of a genuine paysan.

The Swiss

Swiss farmers are tough, independent, resilient, well-prepared for every kind of natural disaster and above all staunchly conservative. These characteristics have been passed on to Swiss town-dwellers, who go about their day as if they too were farming a lonely mountain cliff.

The Germans

Most Germans apply the rule that more equals better. If a passing quip makes you smile, then surely by making it longer the pleasure will be increased. As a rule, if you are cornered by someone keen to give you a laugh, you must expect to miss lunch and most of that afternoon's appointments.

The Italians

Italians grow up knowing that they have to be economical with the truth. All other Italians are, so if they didn't play the game they would be at a serious disadvantage. They have to fabricate to keep one step ahead.

The English

If an English man or woman refers to you as 'a good sport', you will know that you have really arrived. For to them it is a qualification normally never awarded to a foreigner and by no means within the grasp of all the English.

The Americans

A wise traveller realises that a few happy moments with an American do not translate into a permanent commitment of any kind. Indeed, permanent commitments are what Americans fear the most. This is a nation whose most fundamental social relationship is the casual acquaintance.

Comments on Xenophobe's® Guides

On the series:
'Good natured, witty and useful. The Xenophobe's guides to different nations deserves a real cheer.' Reviewer of *The European*

The Greeks:
'This book is brilliant. I have rediscovered myself in many of the sayings in the book and strangely enough, I have also learned a few things too.'

Reader from Greece

The Poles:
'A must for all Poles of all generations everywhere. What superb insight, what humour — but of course written by a Pole.'

Polish reader from England

The Icelanders:
'Spot on. Short, funny, accurate — a good preparation for anybody thinking of living amongst this remarkable set of people.'

Reader from Singapore

The Czechs
'Czech this out if you are headed for Prague. A tongue-in-cheek guide to the bewildering Czechs which provides information and insight.' Reader from the USA

Xenophobe's® guides

Available as printed books and e-books:

Xenophobe's® lingo learners

Xenophobe's Guides

Xenophobe's® Guides are available
as e-books from Amazon, iBookstore, and
other online sources, and via:

www.xenophobes.com

Xenophobe's® Guides print versions
can be purchased through online retailers
(Amazon, etc.) or via our web site:

www.xenophobes.com

In the US contact:
IPG Trafalgar Square, Chicago

toll free no: 1-800-888-4741
e-mail: orders@ipgbook.com

In the UK, contact Xenophobe's® Guides

telephone: +44 (0)20 7733 8585
e-mail: info@xenophobes.com

Xenophobe's® Guides
5 St John's Buildings
Canterbury Crescent
London SW9 7QH

Payment can be made with Visa or Mastercard.
Postage and packing is FREE in the UK for orders of
more than one book (to one address).

Xenophobe's Guides